tra

TERRY WINN

First published in 2003 by New Holland Publishers (NZ) Ltd
Auckland · Sydney · London · Cape Town

218 Lake Road, Northcote, Auckland, New Zealand
14 Aquatic Drive, Frenchs Forest, NSW 2086, Australia
86 Edgware Road, London W2 2EA, United Kingdom
80 McKenzie Street, Cape Town 8001, South Africa

www.newhollandpublishers.com

ISBN: 1 86966 040 4 (soft cover)

ISBN: 1 86966 050 1 (hard cover)

Publishing manager: Renée Lang
Design: Trevor Newman

A catalogue record for this book is available from the National Library of New Zealand.

10 9 8 7 6 5 4 3 2 1

Colour reproduction by SC (Sang Choy) International Pte Ltd, Singapore
Printed in China through Phoenix Offset, Hong Kong

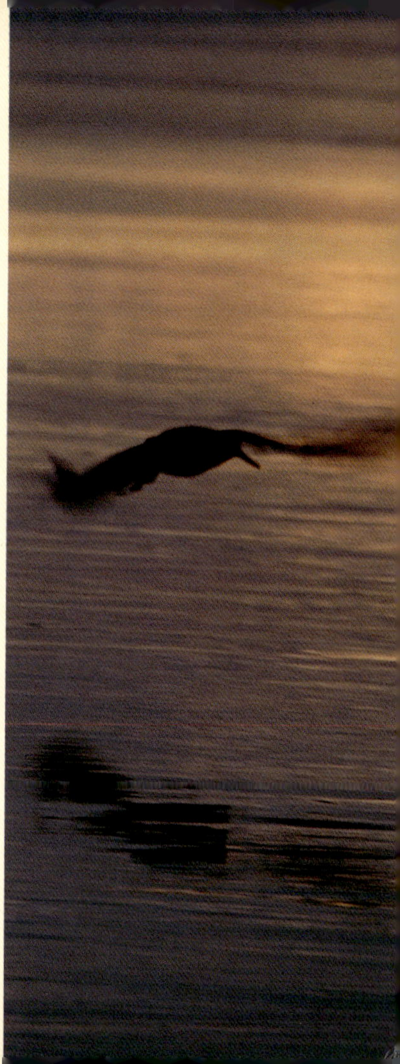

Alone we can do so little;

together we can do so much.

Helen Keller

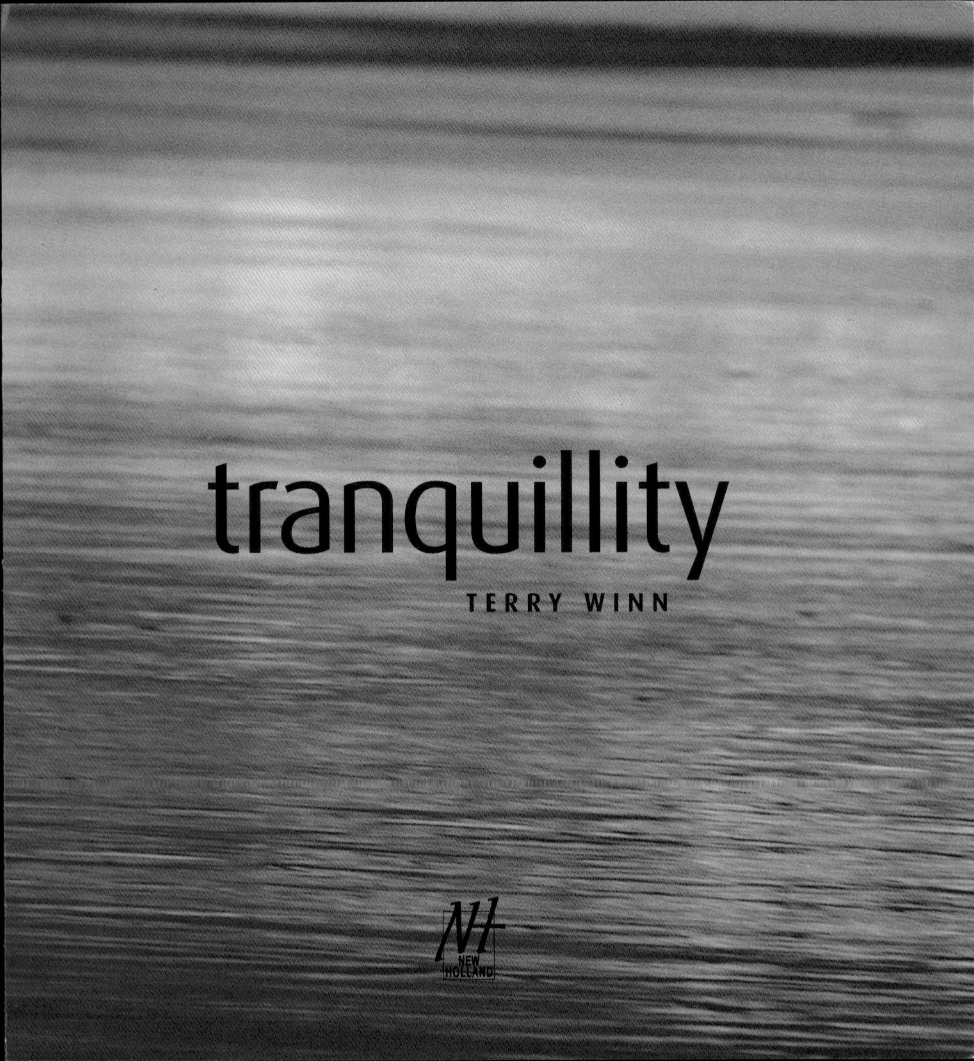

tranquillity

TERRY WINN

NEW HOLLAND

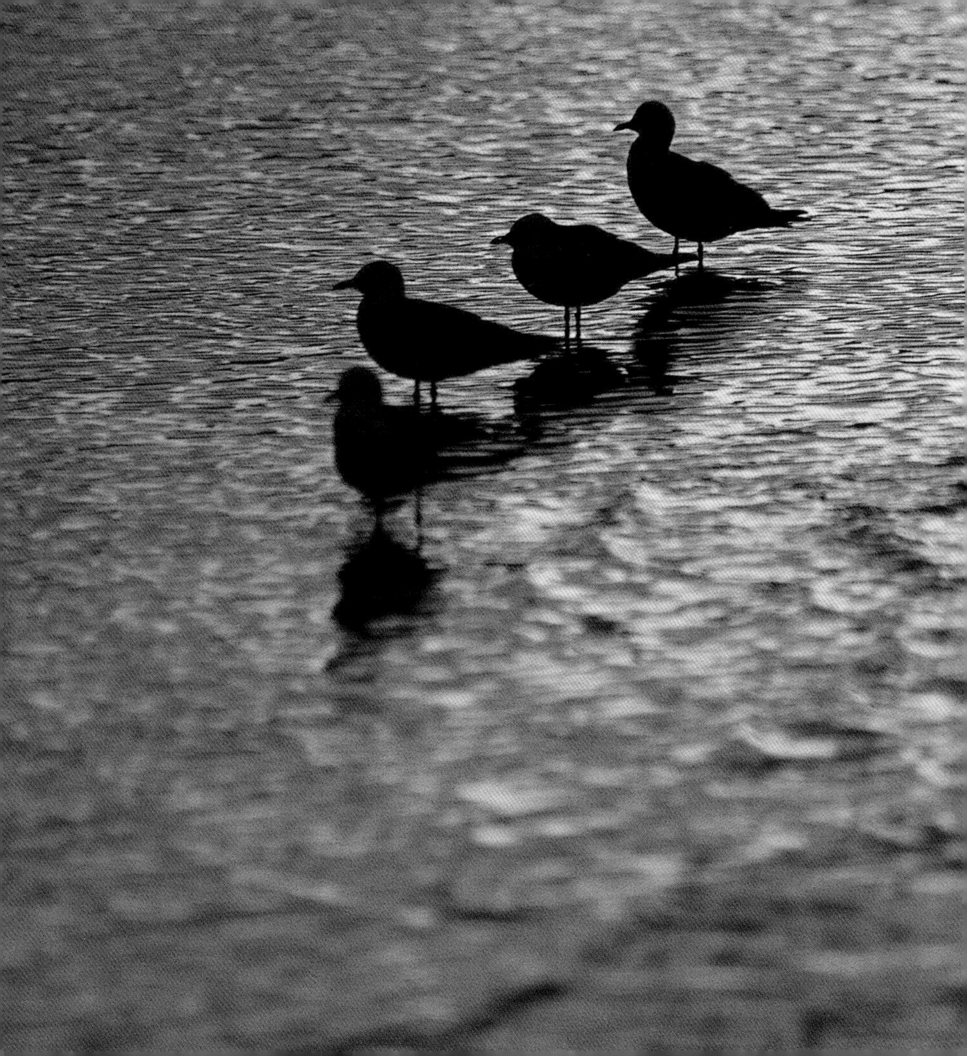

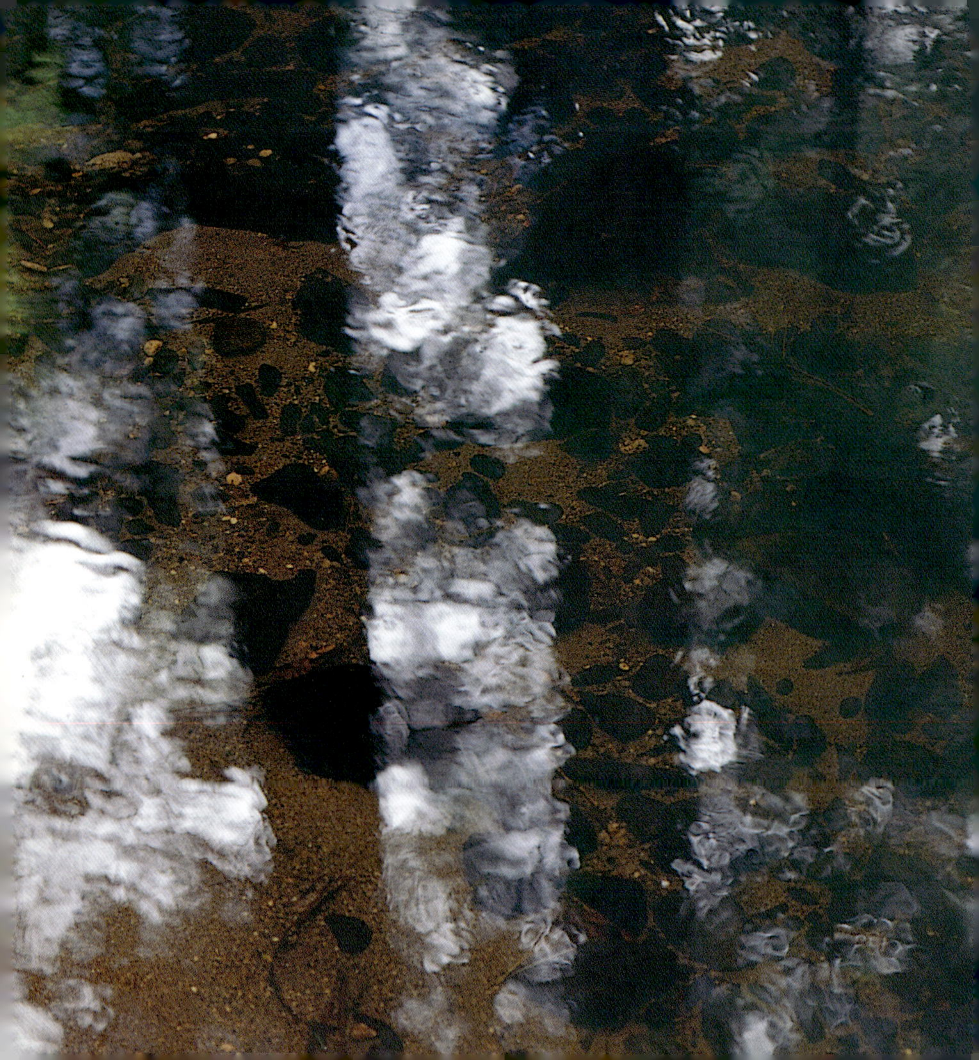

Joy in looking and comprehending is

Nature's most beautiful gift.

Albert Einstein

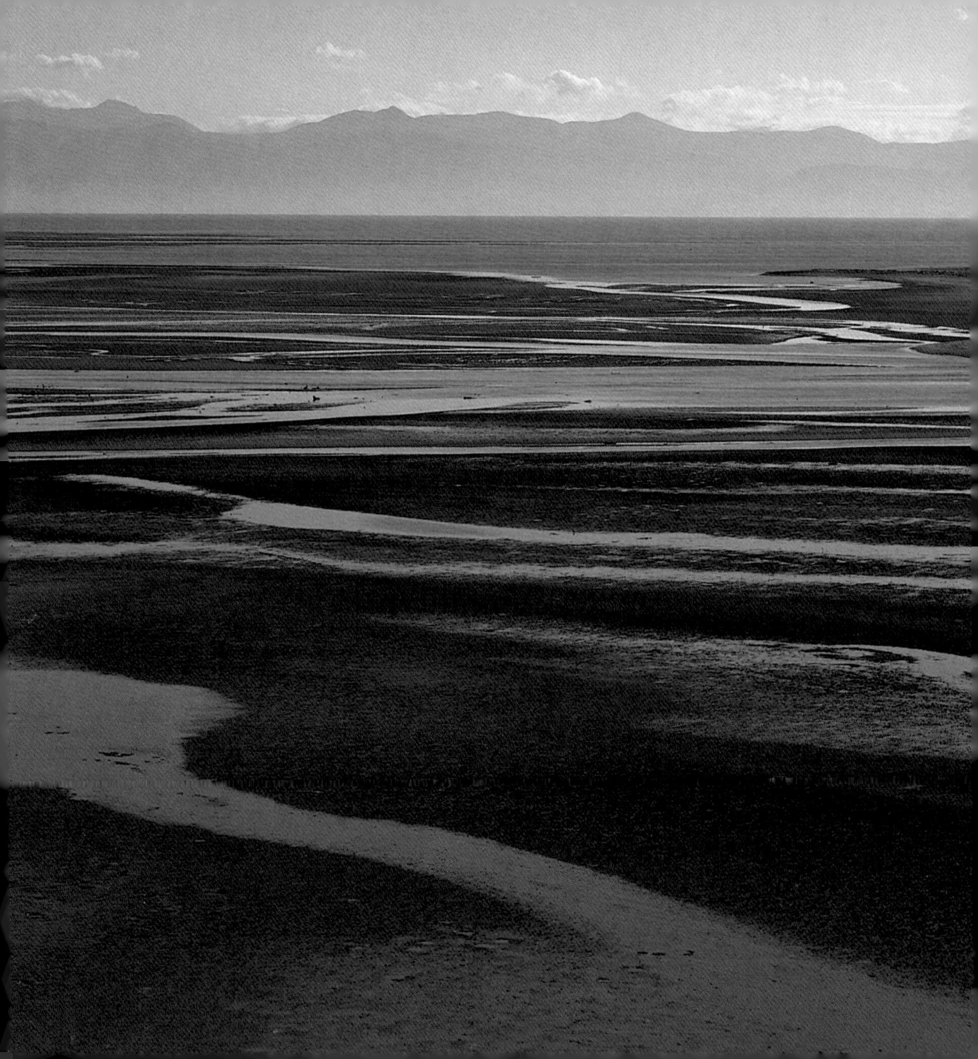

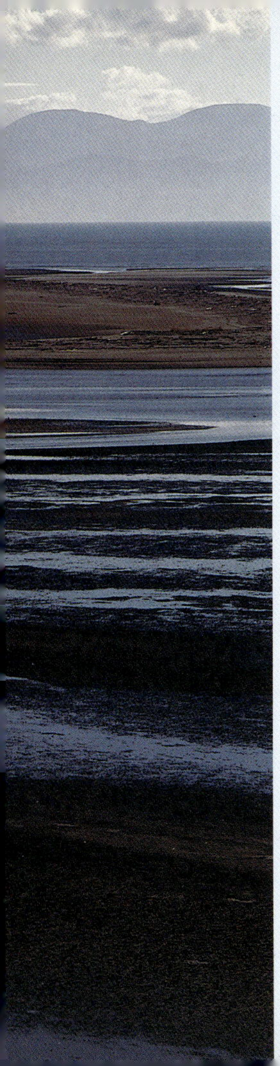

In every out-thrust headland,
in every curving beach,
in every grain of sand
there is a story
of the earth.

Rachel Carson

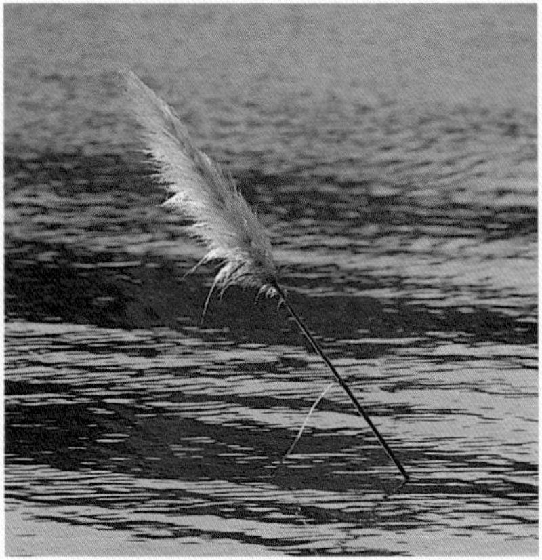

Learn to get in touch with
the silence within yourself

and know that everything
in life has a purpose.

ELIZABETH KÜBLER-ROSS

In all things of nature
there is something of the marvellous.

Aristotle

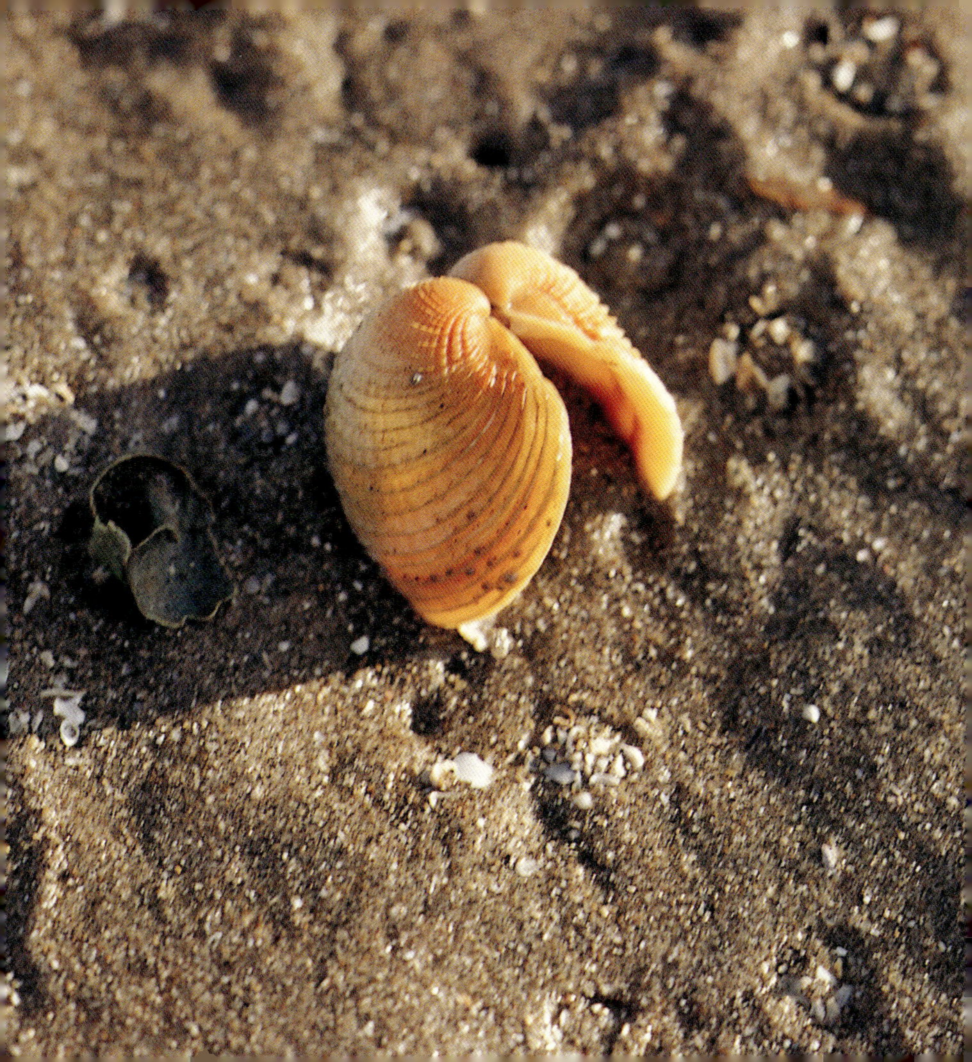

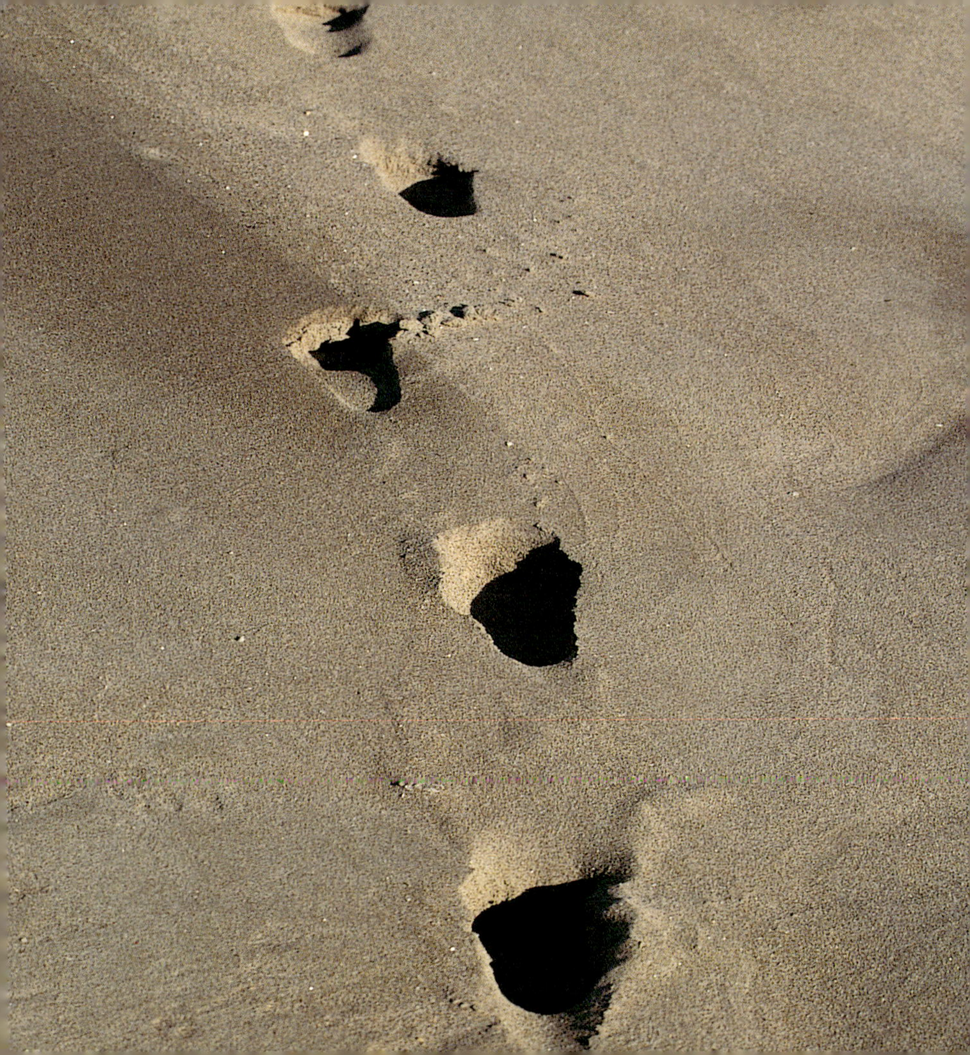

Do not go where the path may lead,

go instead where
there is no path

and leave a trail.

Ralph Waldo Emerson

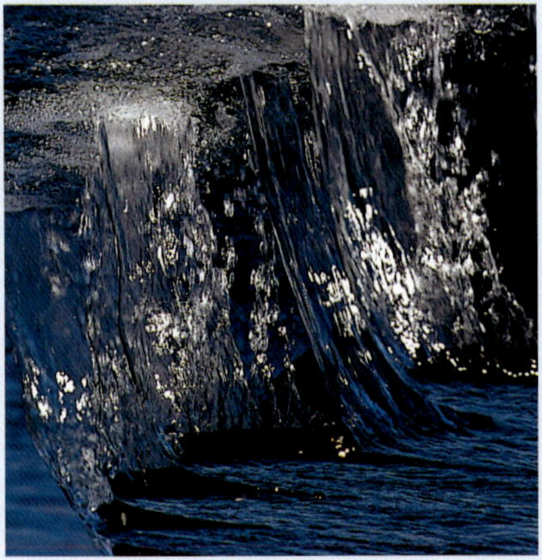

Like water,
be gentle and strong.

Be gentle enough
to follow the natural paths of the earth,
and strong enough
to rise up and reshape the world.

Renda Peterson

Think of all the beauty
still left around you and
be happy.

Anne Frank

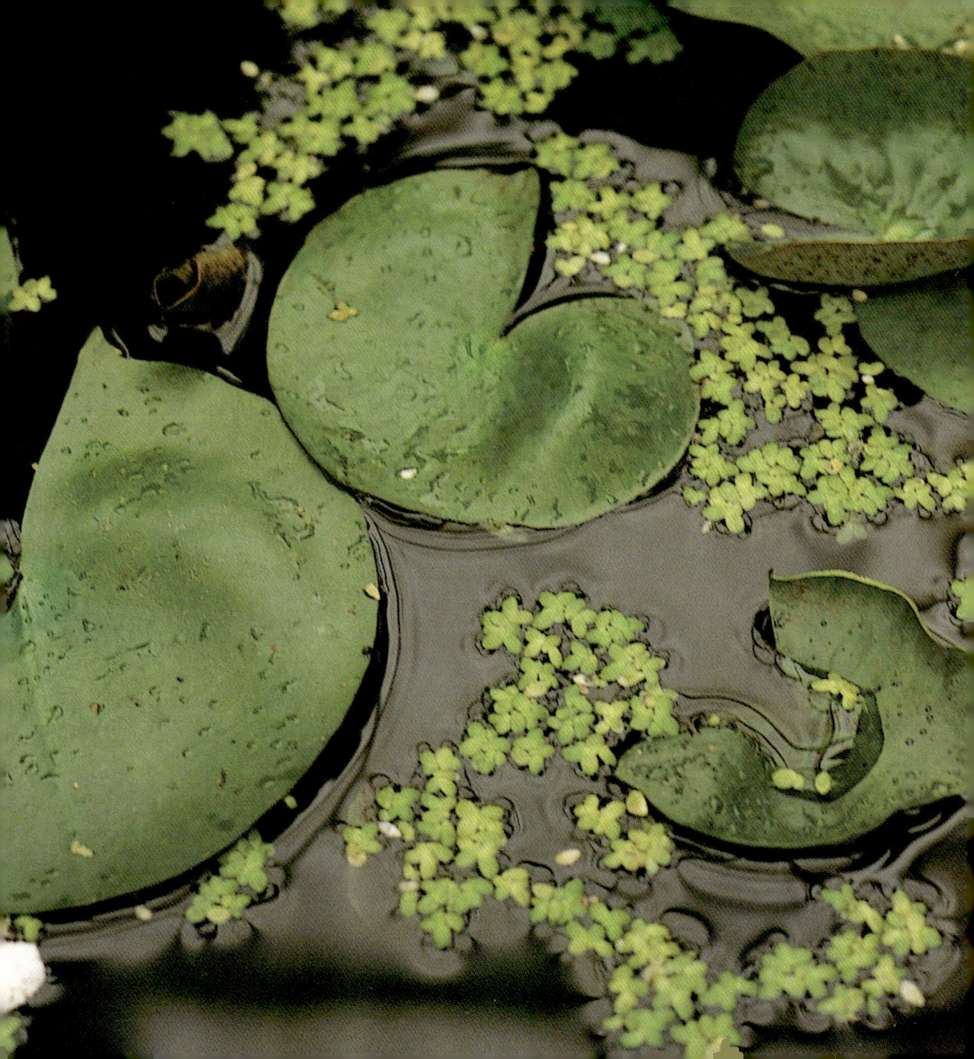

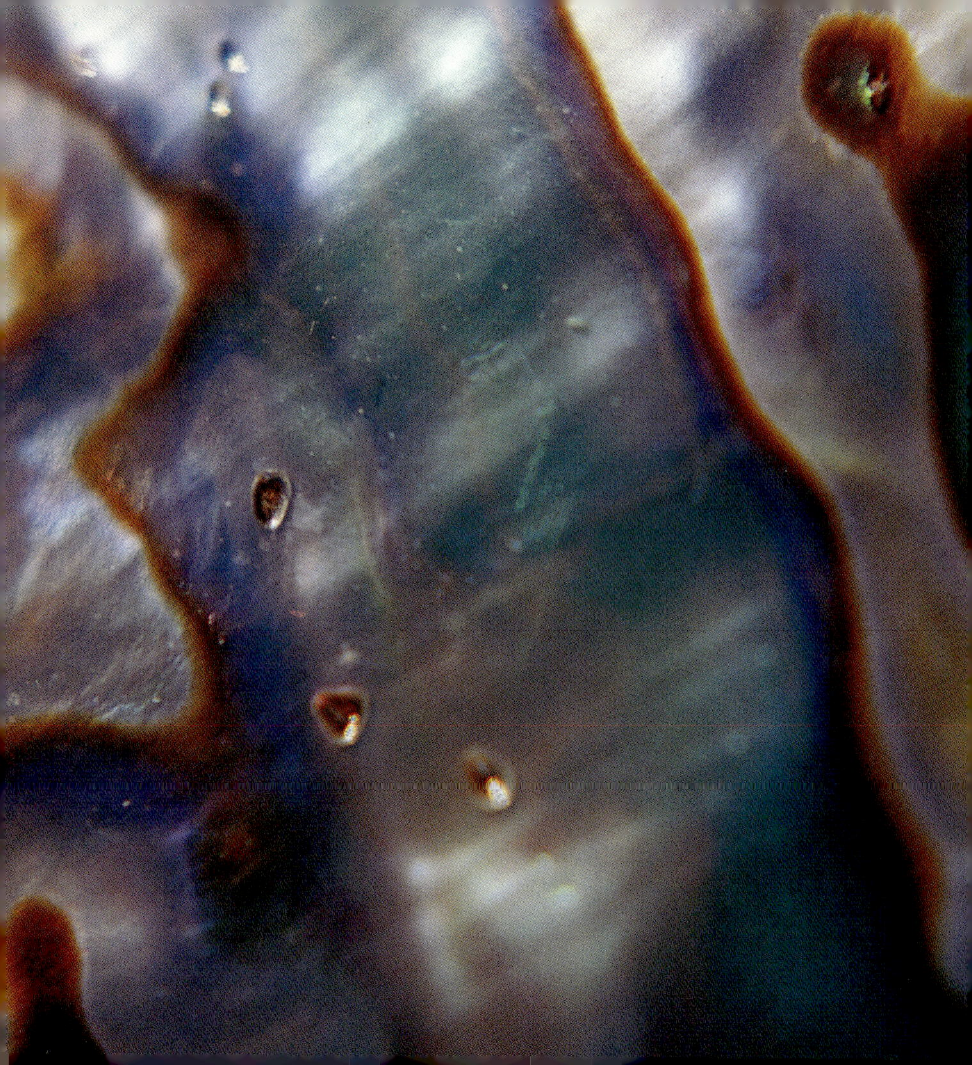

When love and skill work together,
expect a masterpiece.

JOHN RUSKIN

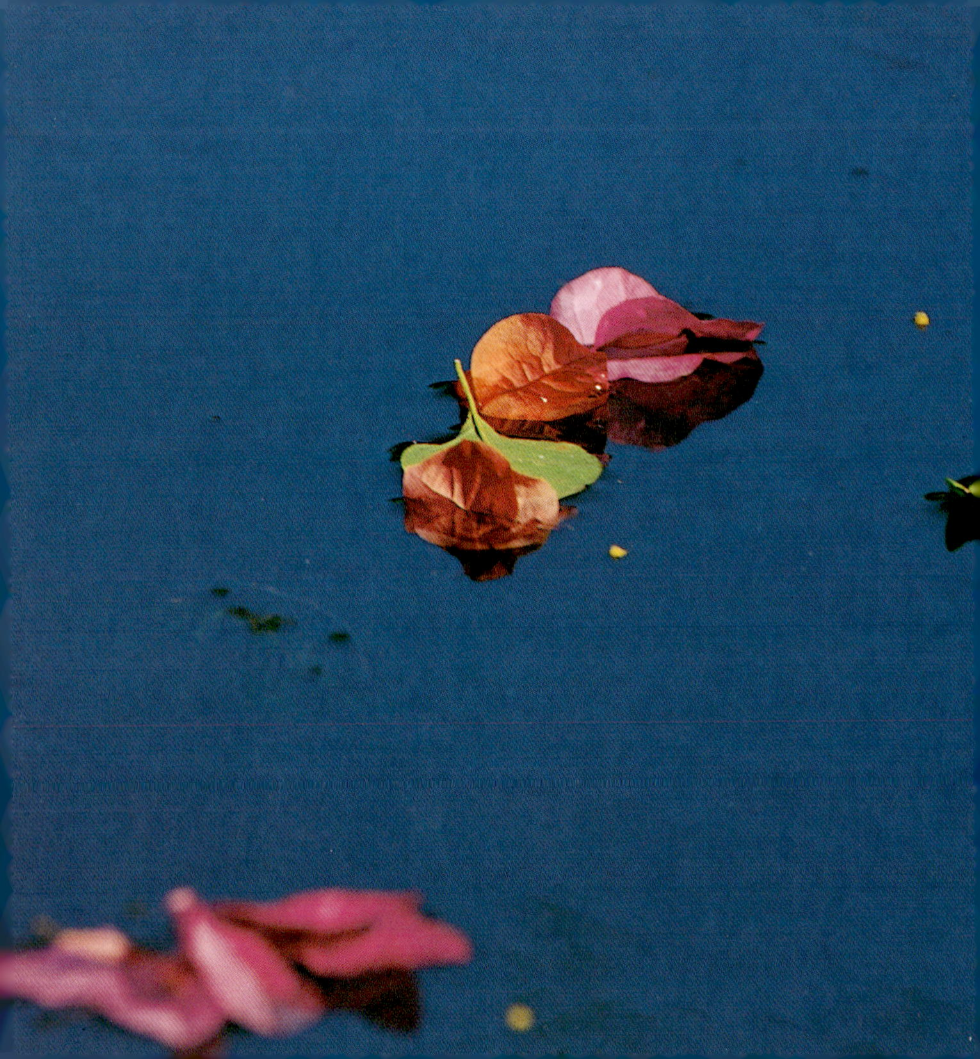

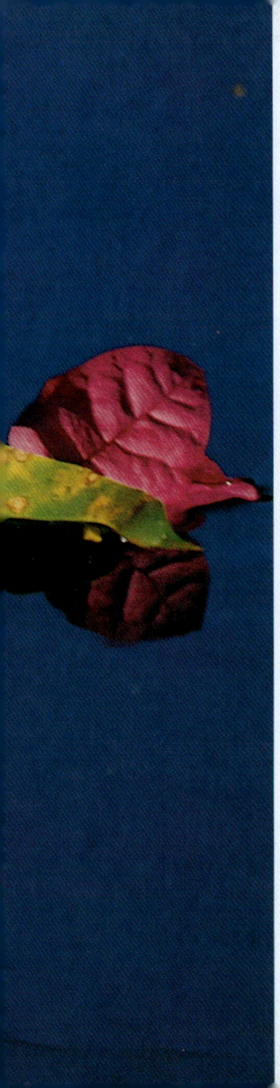

Do not fear to hope...
Each time we smell the autumn's
dying scent, we know that
primrose time
will come again.

Samuel Taylor Coleridge

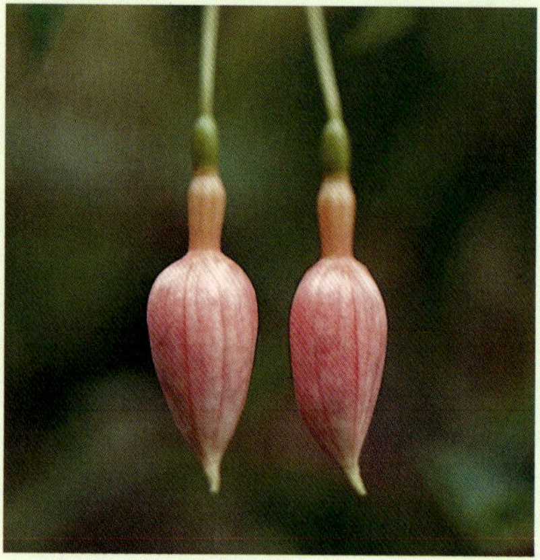

To treat life
as less than a miracle
is to give up on it.

Wendall Berry

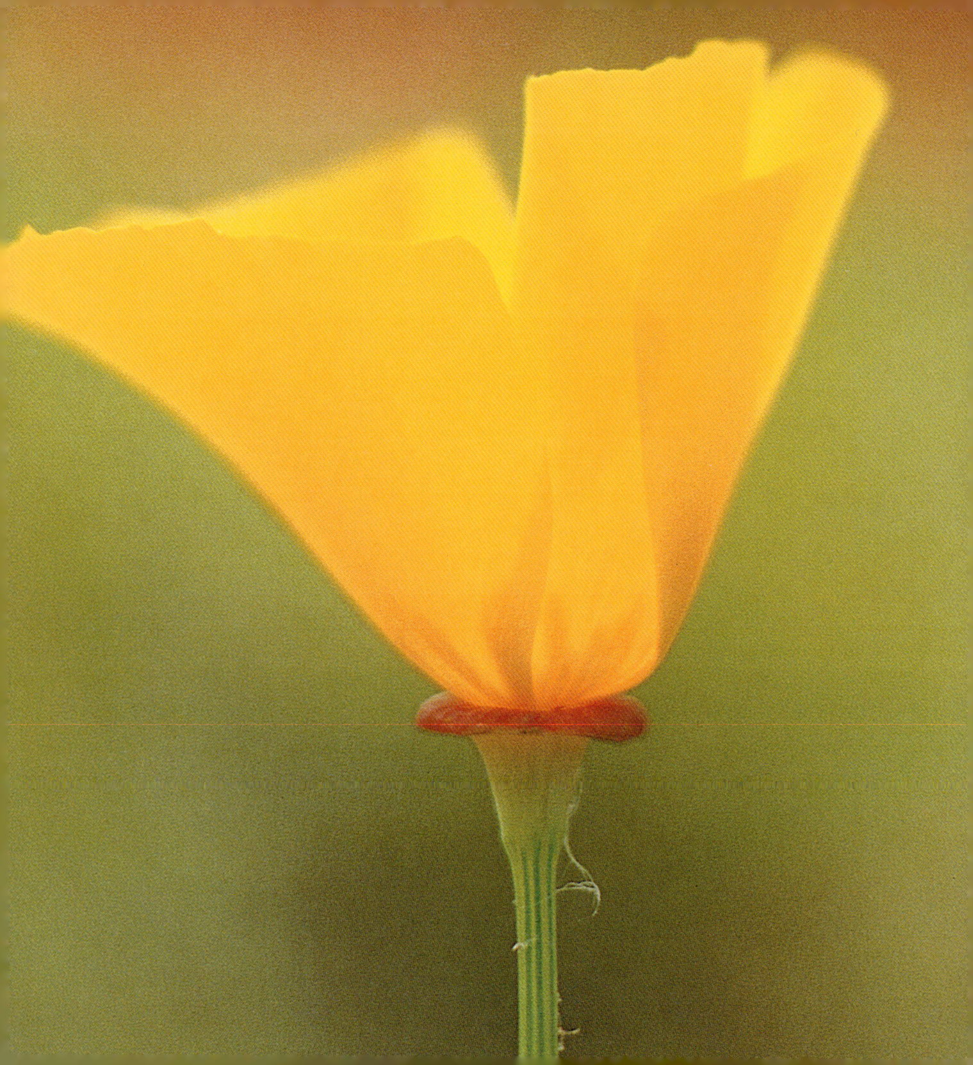

Every flower is a soul
blossoming in Nature.

Gerard de Nerval

Every blade of grass
has its Angel
that bends over it and whispers,
'Grow, grow.'

The Talmud

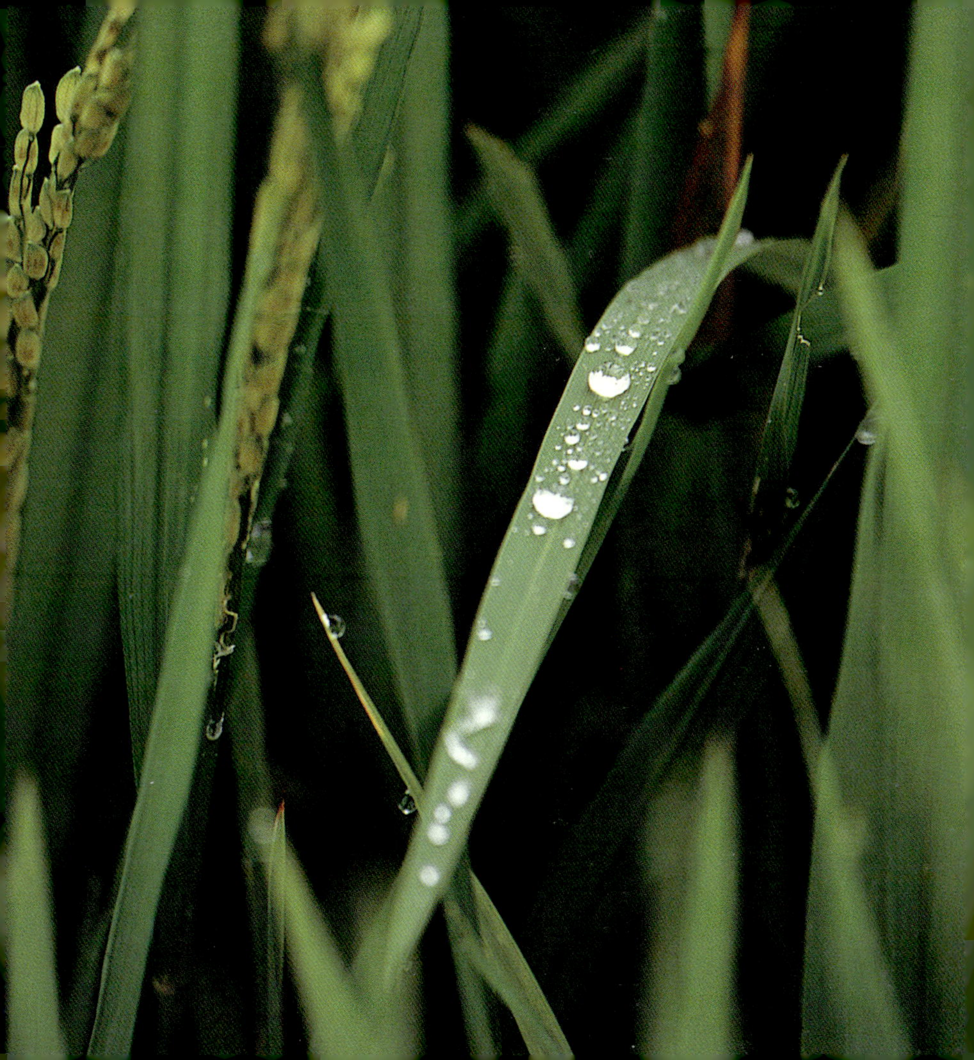

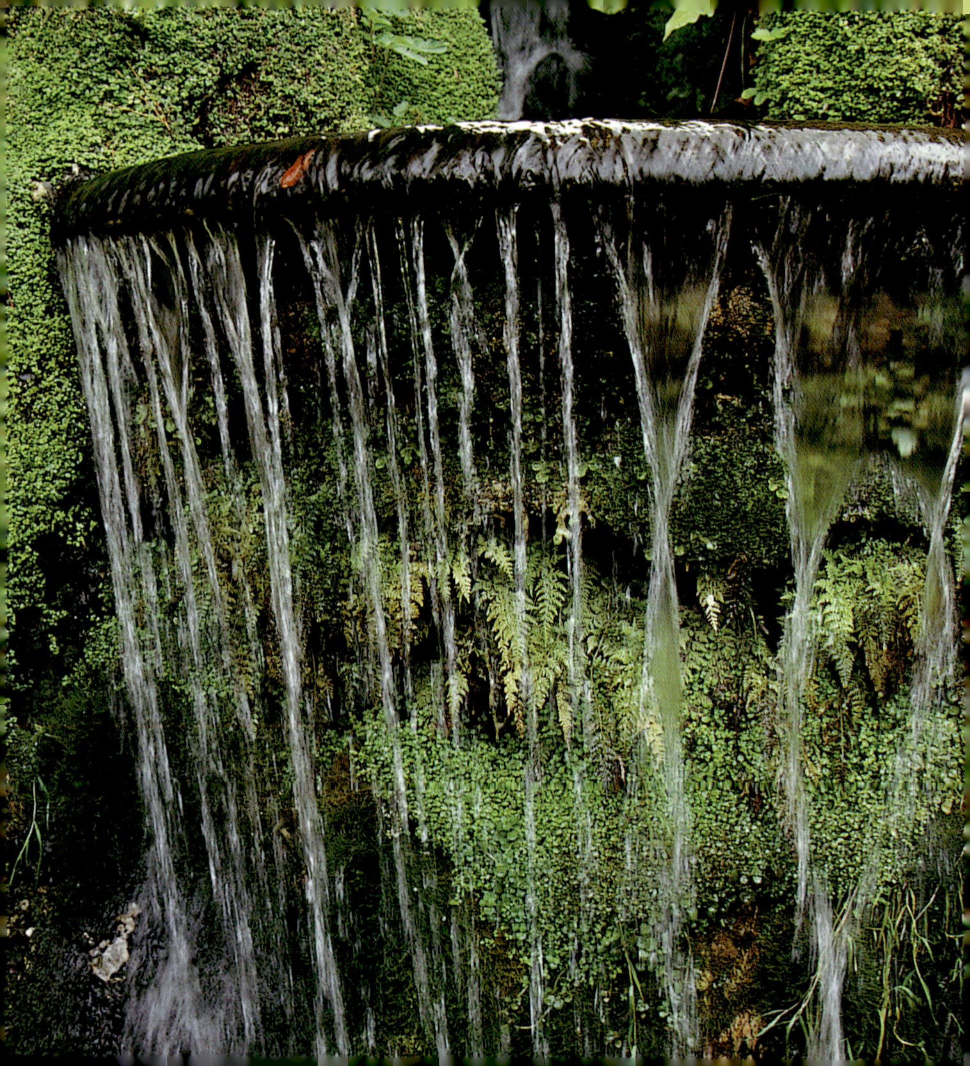

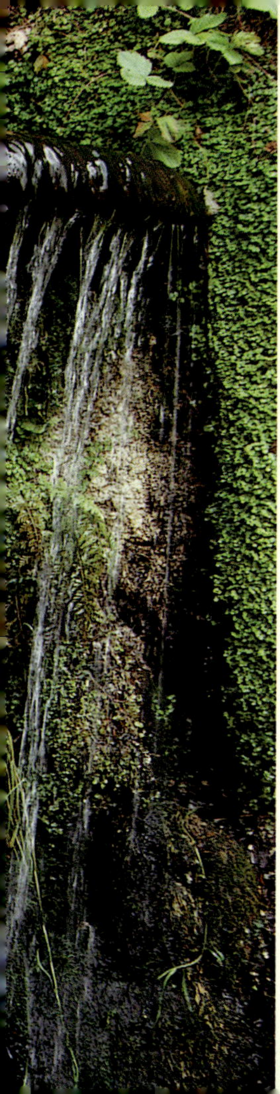

The world
is not to be put in order;
the world is order,
incarnate.
It is for us to
harmonise
with this order.

Henry Miller

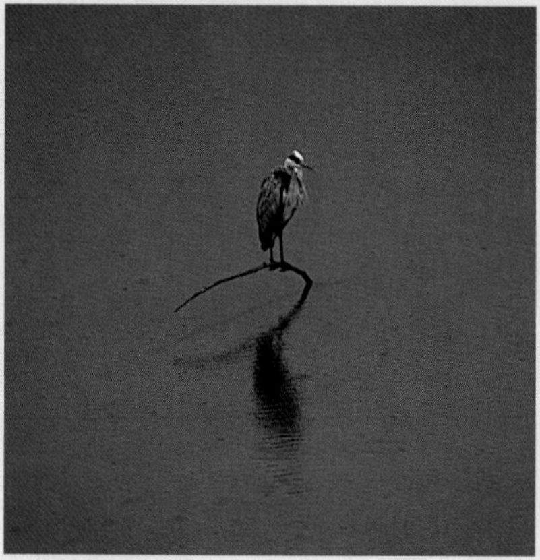

He who knows others is wise;

He who knows himself is enlightened.

LAO-TZU

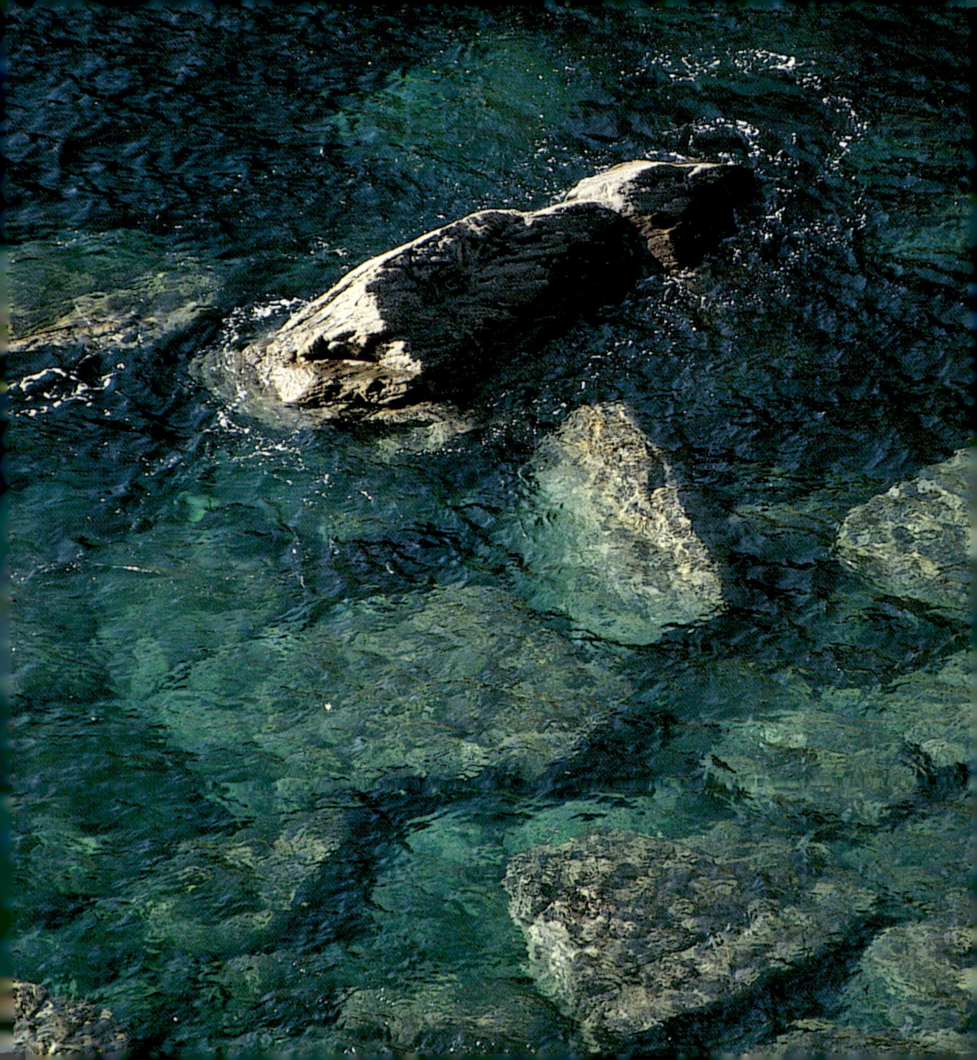

It is neither wealth nor splendour;

but tranquillity and occupation

which give you happiness.

THOMAS JEFFERSON

Yesterday is but
today's memory
and tomorrow is
today's dream.

KAHLIL GIBRAN

The mystery of the world
is the visible,
not the invisible.

Oscar Wilde

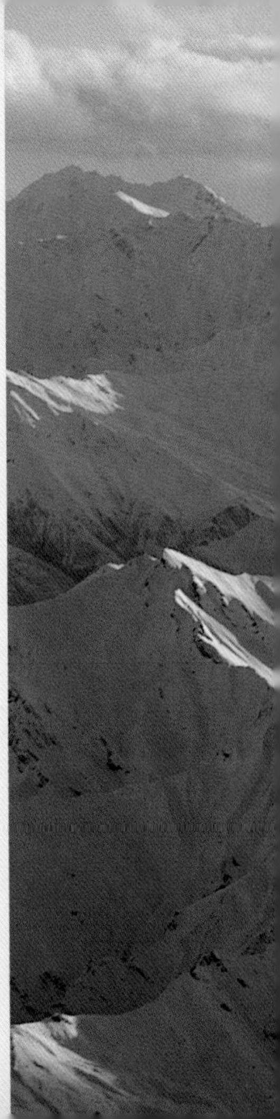

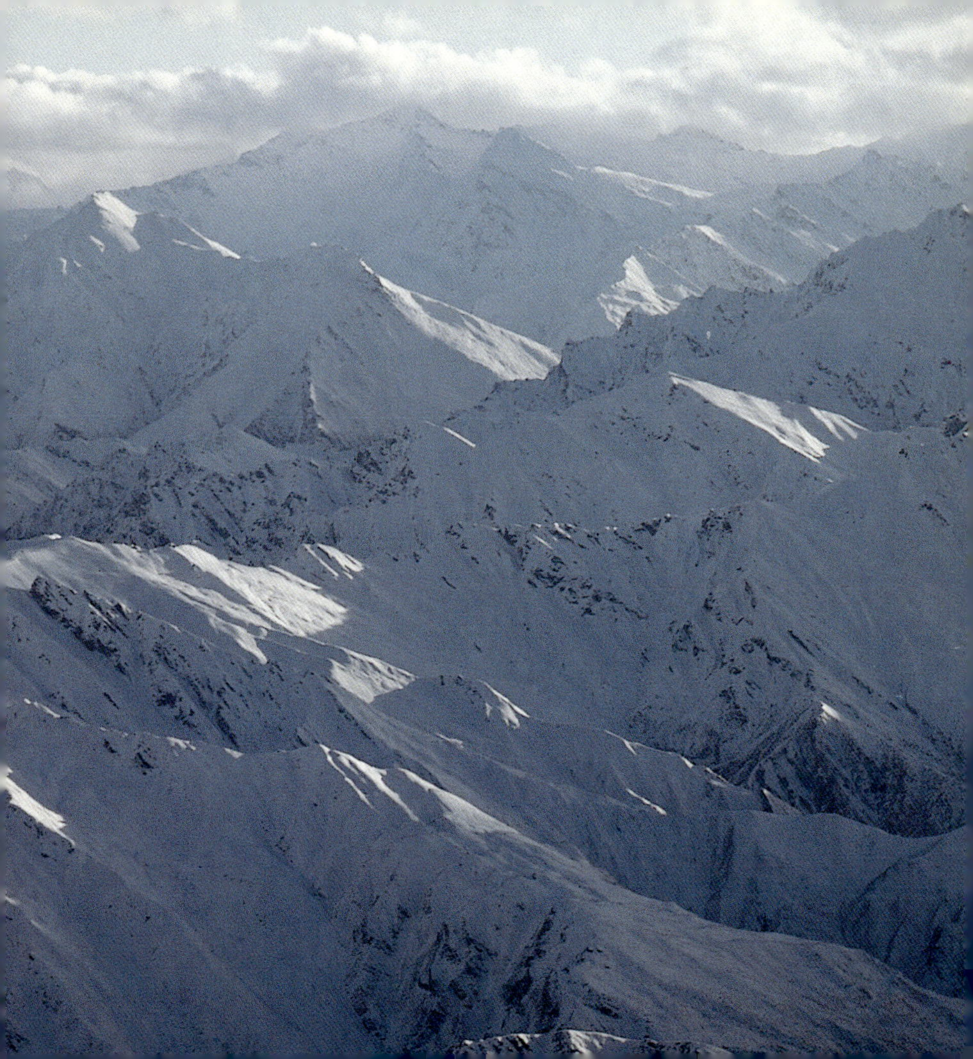

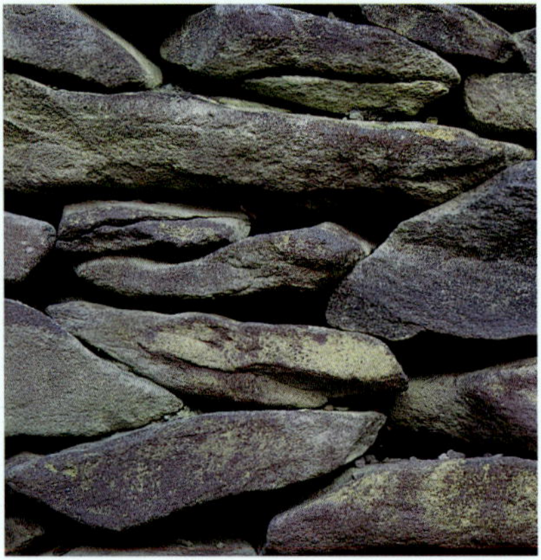

Patience is the companion of wisdom.

ST AUGUSTINE

Adopt the pace of nature:
her secret is patience.

Ralph Waldo Emerson

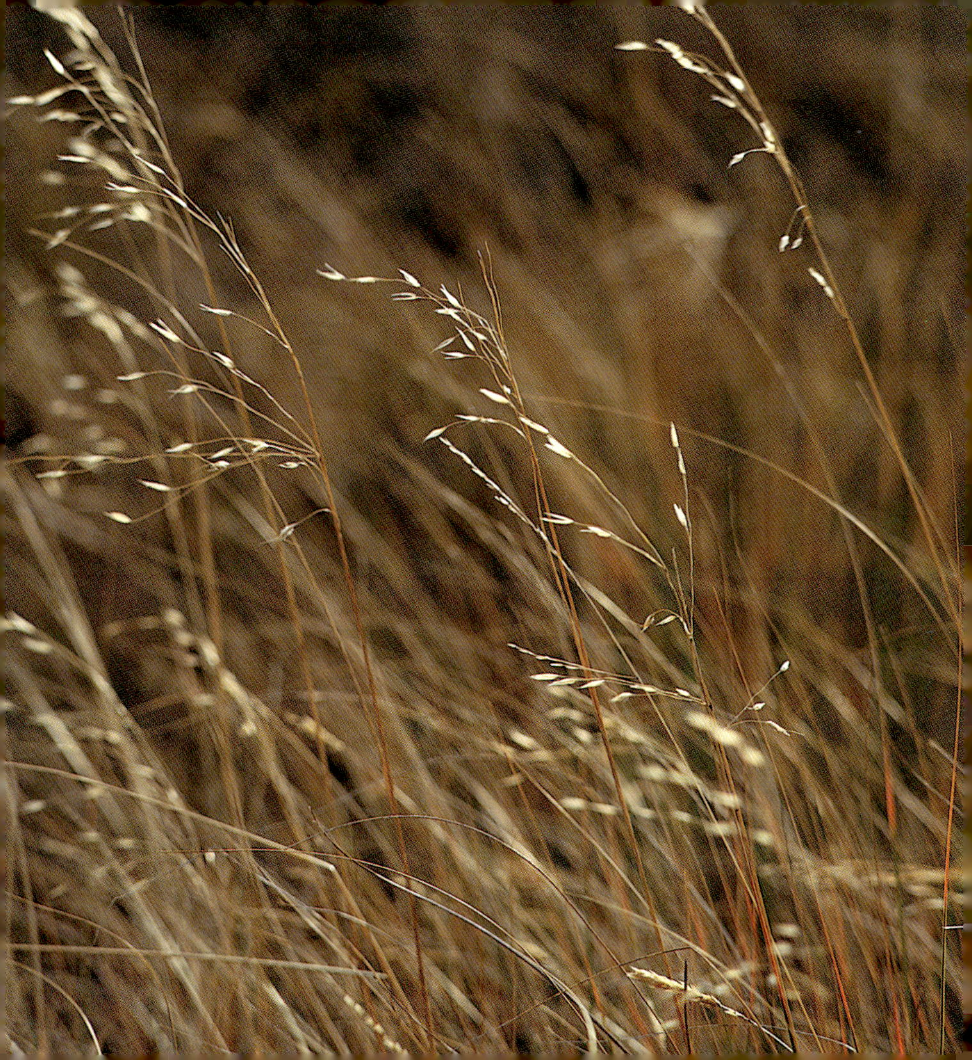

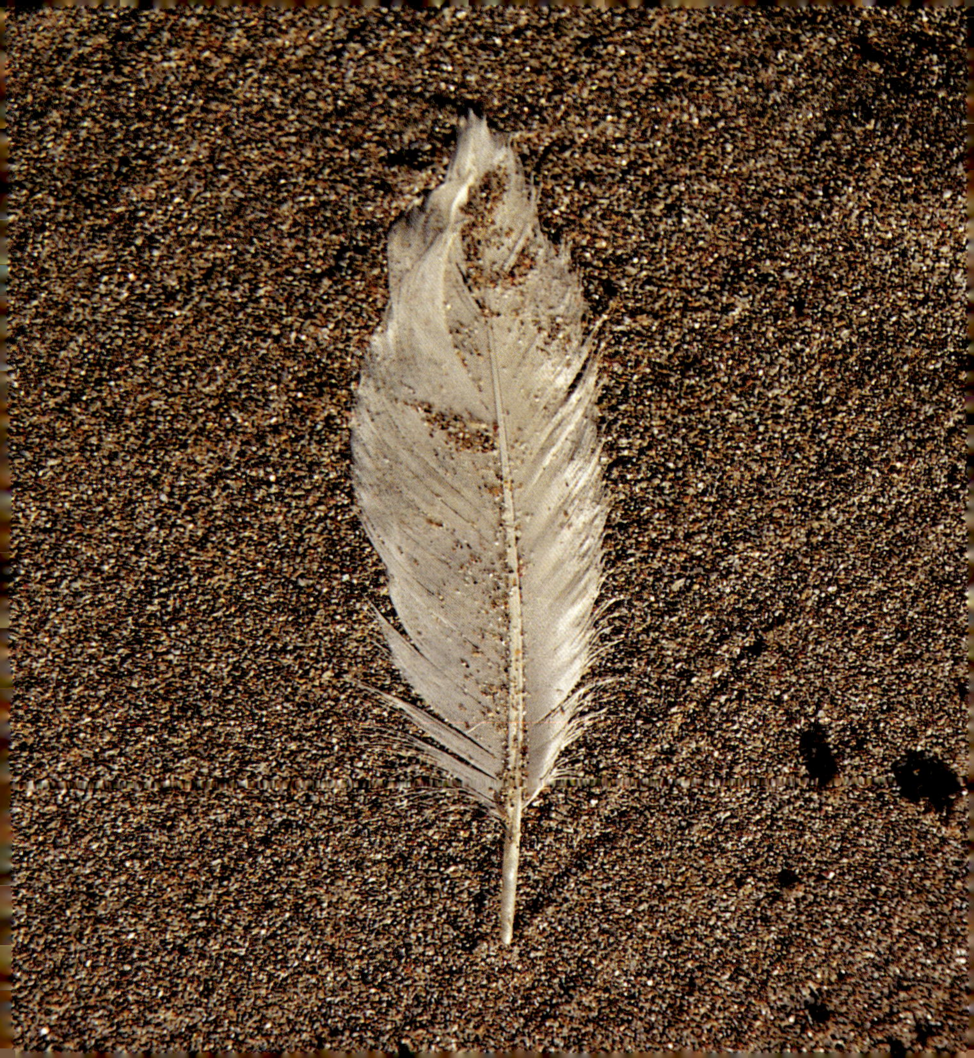

Beauty in things exists
in the mind
which contemplates them.

David Hume

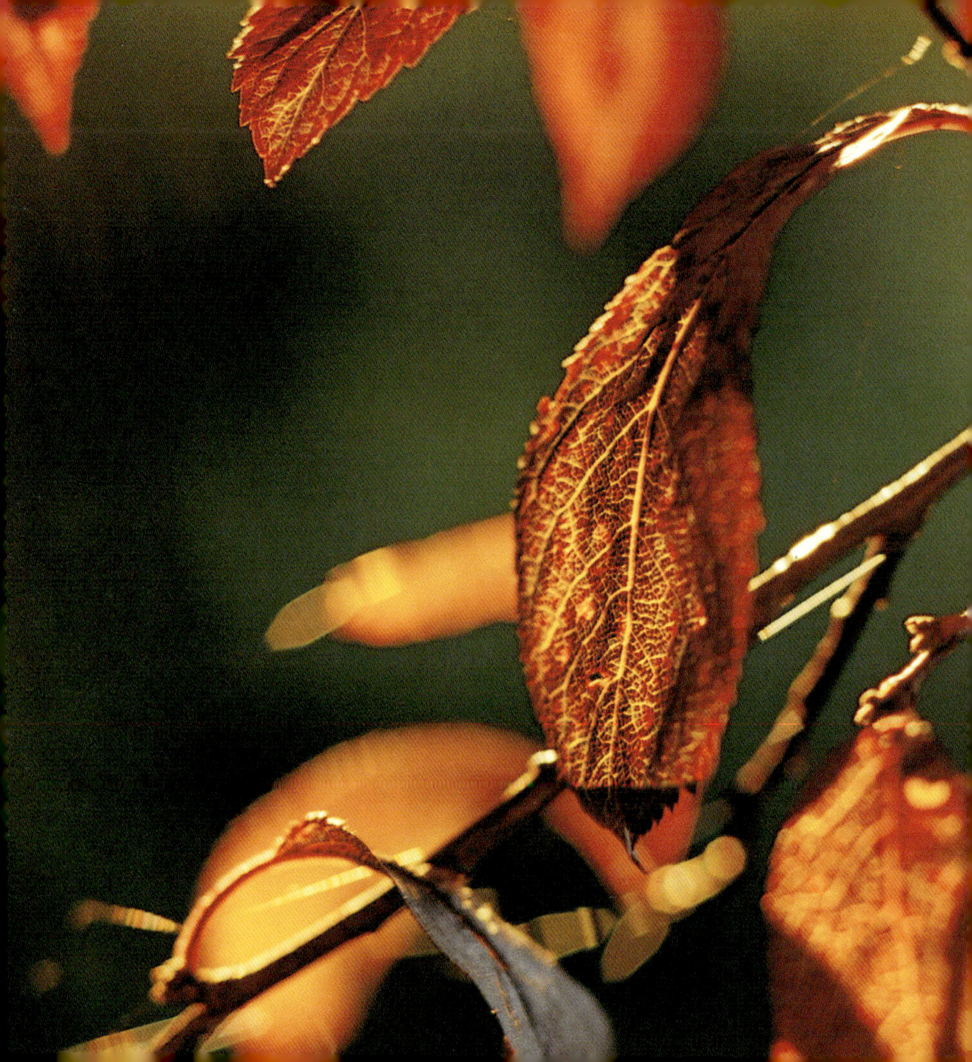

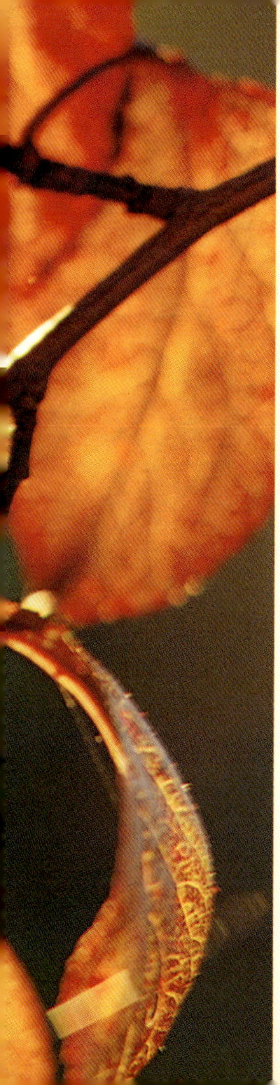

Autumn is
a second spring
when every leaf's a flower.

Albert Camus

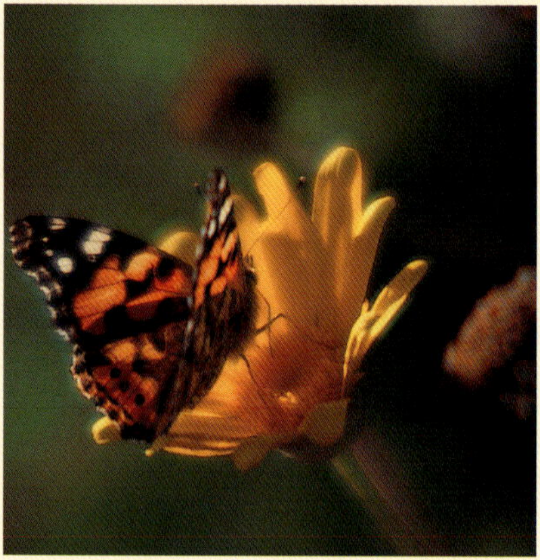

We must not allow the clock

and the calendar to blind us to the fact that

each moment of life is
a miracle and mystery.

H G Wells

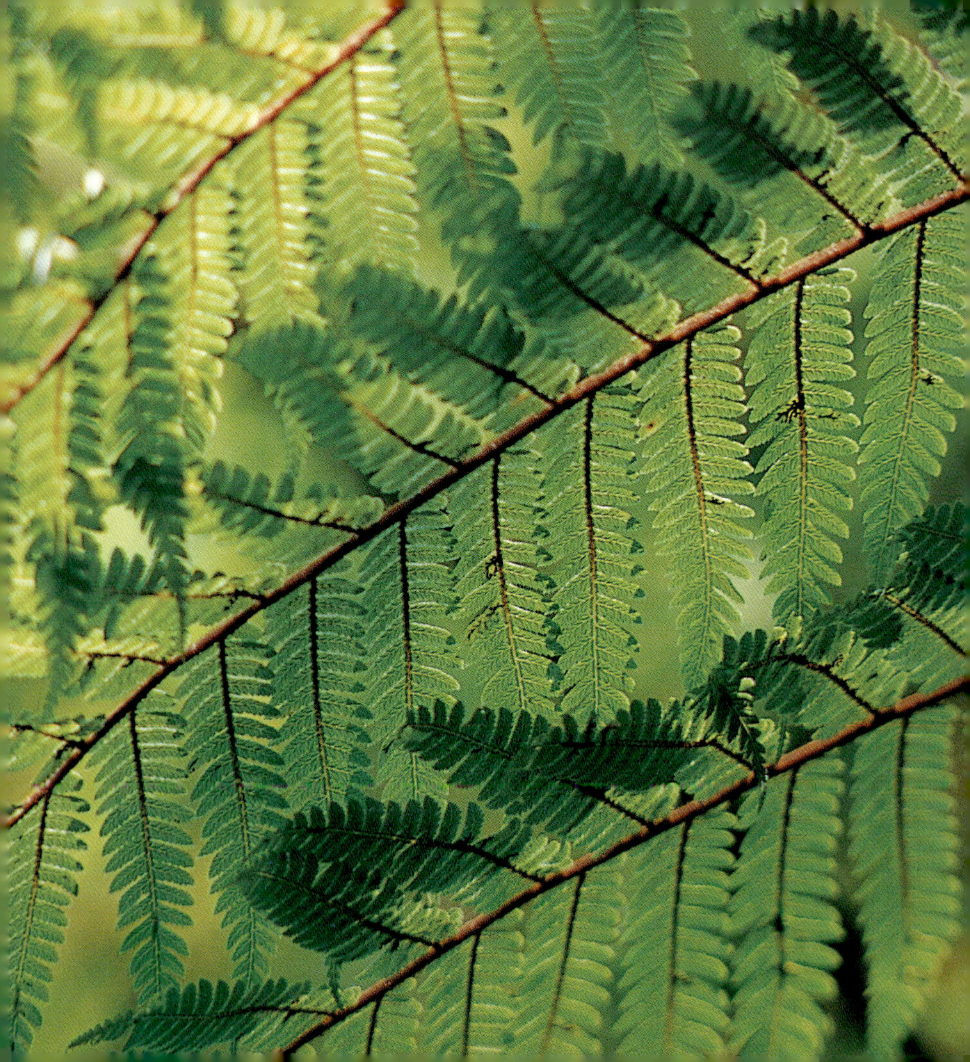

Study nature, love nature,
stay close to nature.
It will never fail you.

Frank Lloyd Wright

I often think

the night is more alive

and more richly coloured

than the day.

Vincent Van Gogh

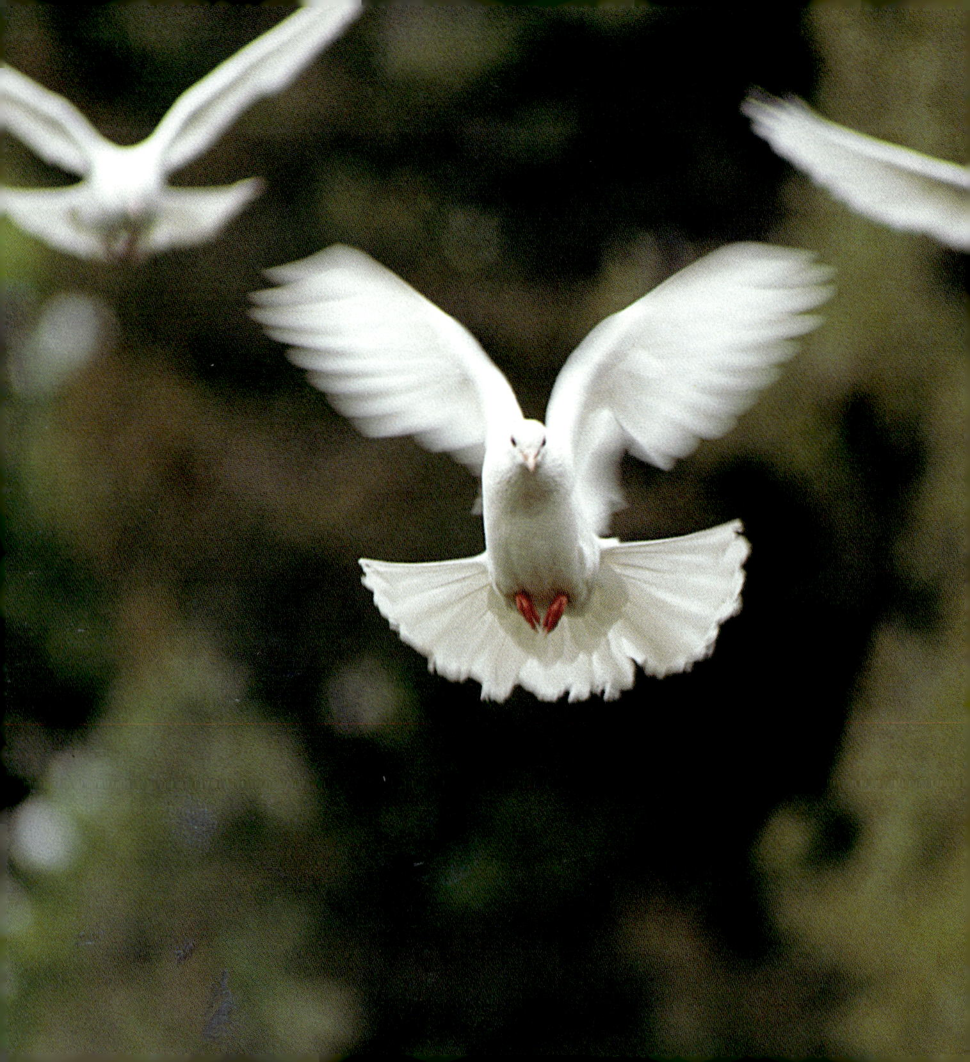

Nothing is
worth more than
this day.
You cannot
relive yesterday.
Tomorrow is still beyond
your reach.

Johann Wolfgang von Goethe

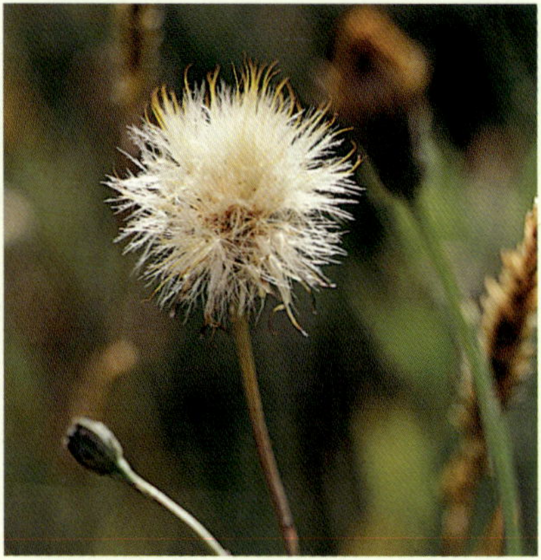

To see a world in a grain of sand

and heaven in a wild flower,

Hold infinity in the palm of your hand

and eternity in an hour.

William Blake

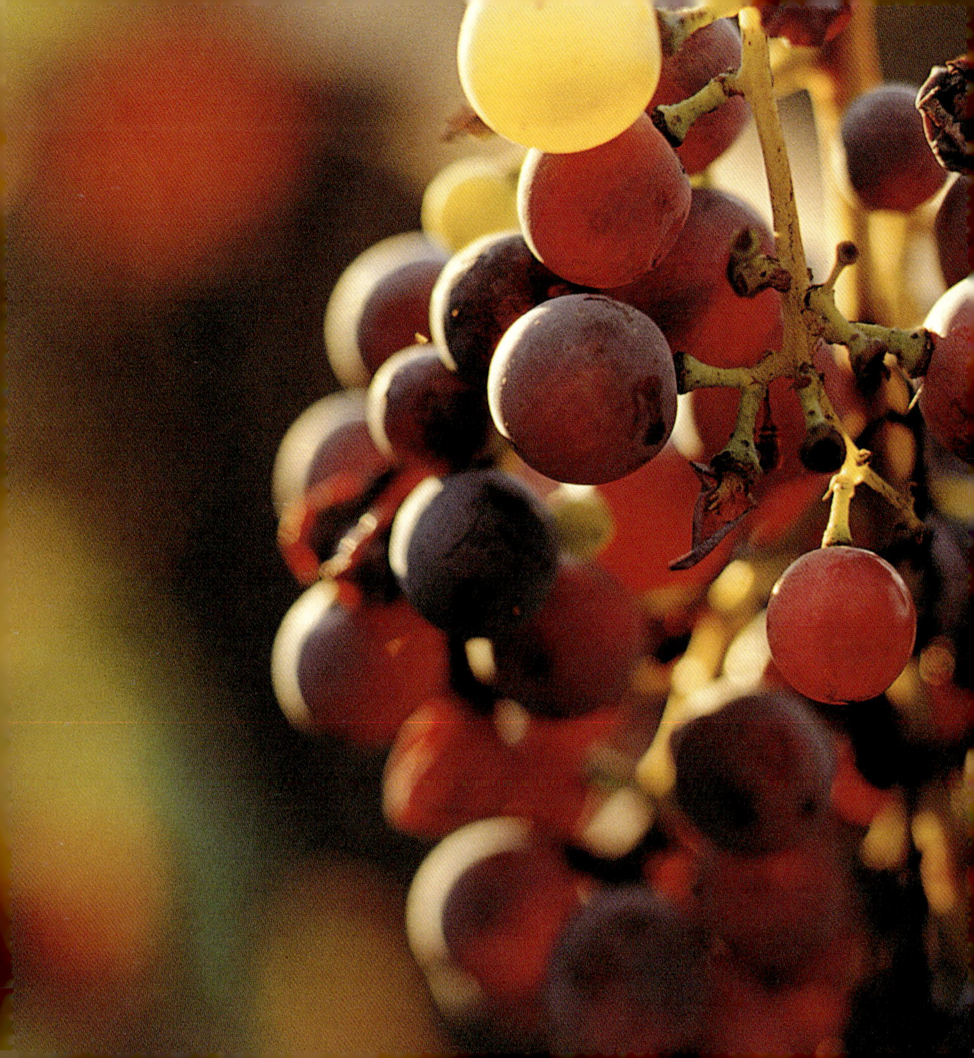

Live each season as it passes;

breathe the air, drink the drink,

taste the fruit...

HENRY DAVID THOREAU

Beauty awakens the soul to act.

Dante Alighieri

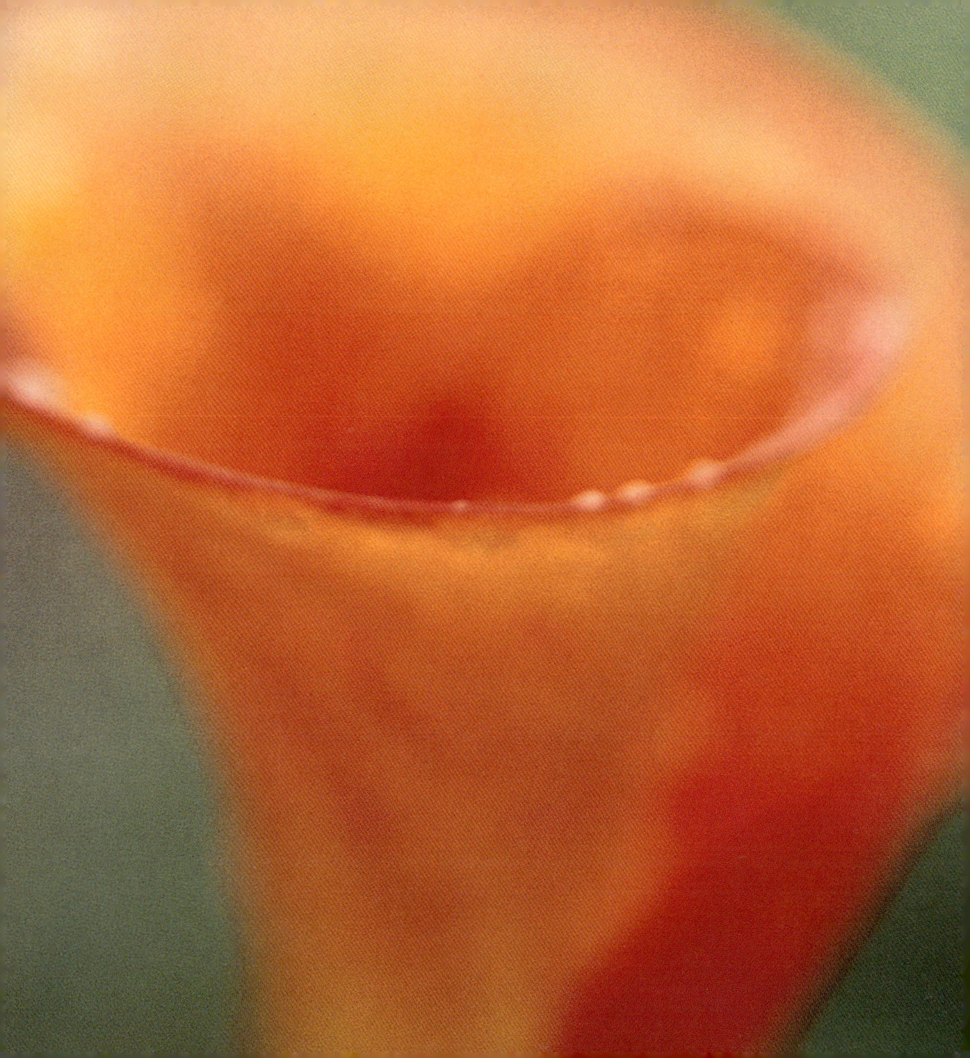

The future belongs to those who believe in the beauty of their dreams.

Eleanor Roosevelt

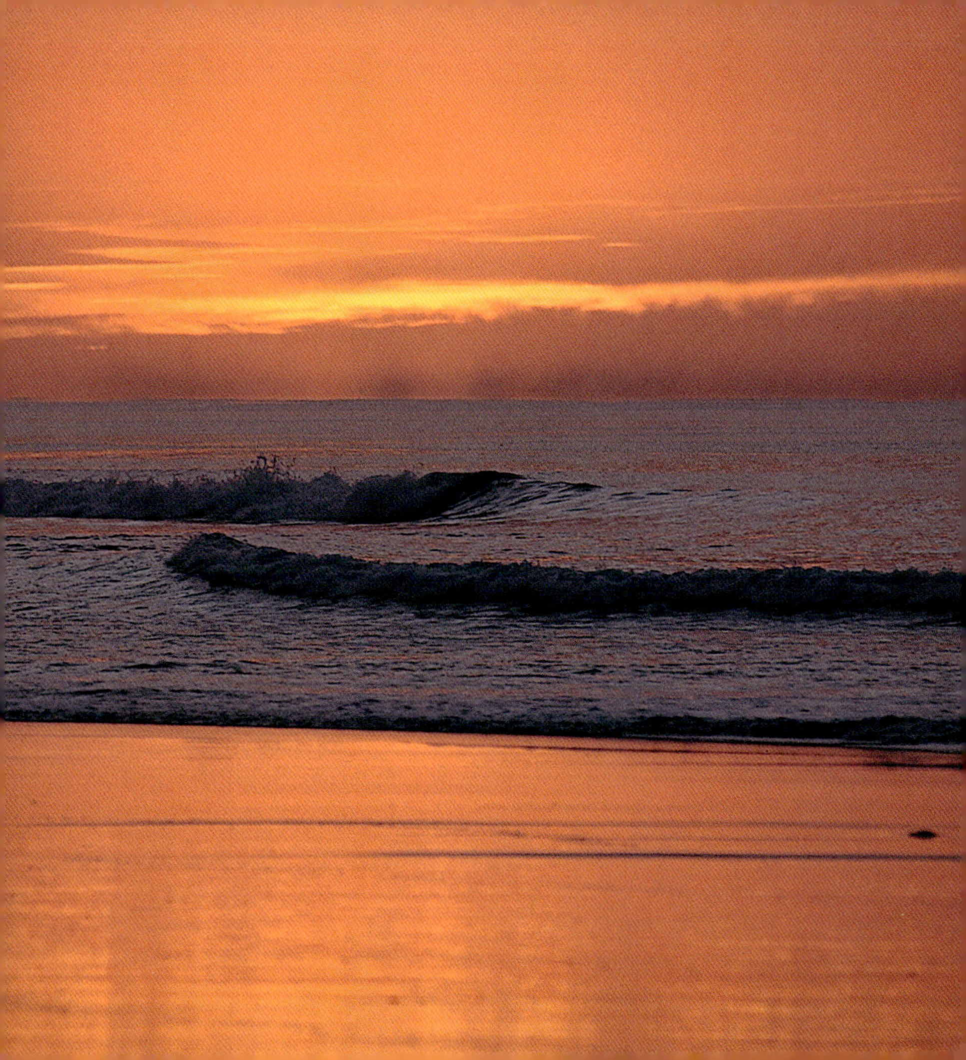

There are places and moments

in which one is so completely alone

that one sees the world entire.

Jules Renard

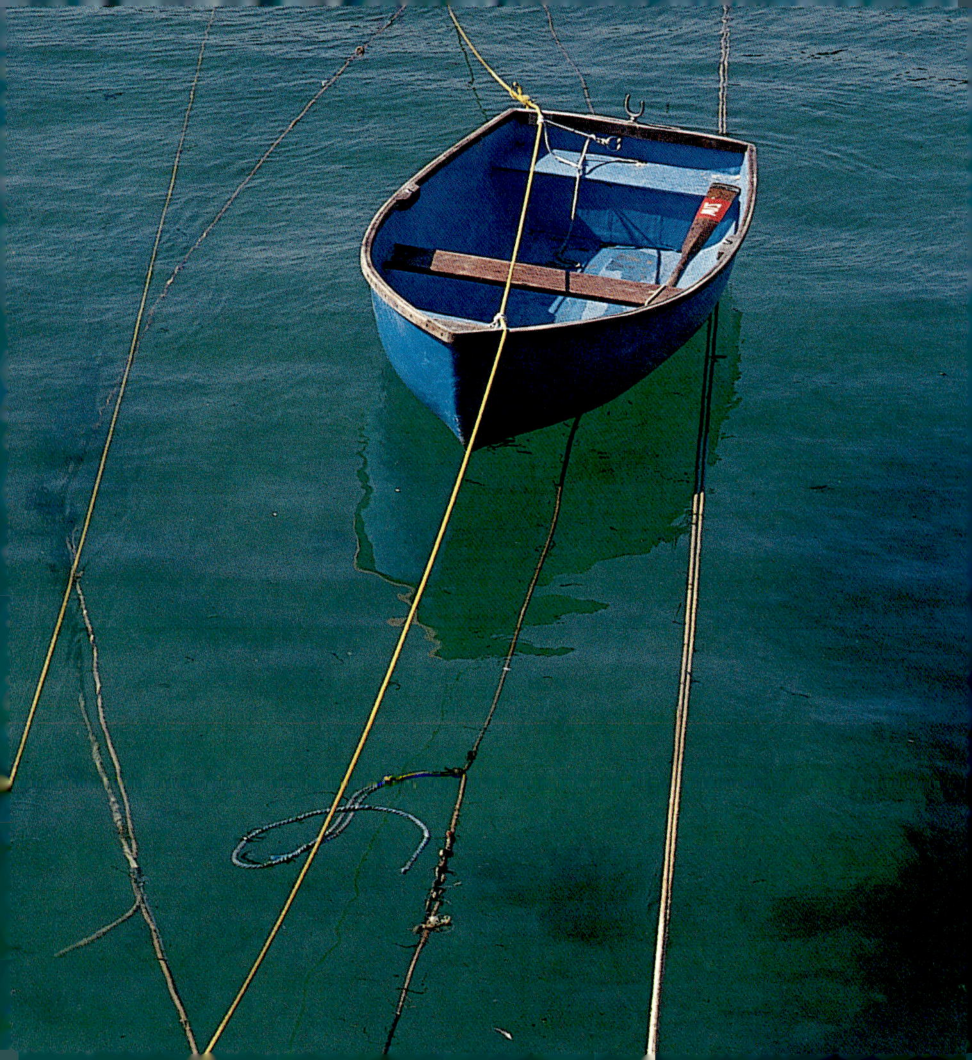

Everything flows and nothing stays.

Heraclitus

Slow down and enjoy life.
It's not only the scenery
you miss by going too fast –
you also miss
the sense of where
you are going and why.

Eddie Cantor

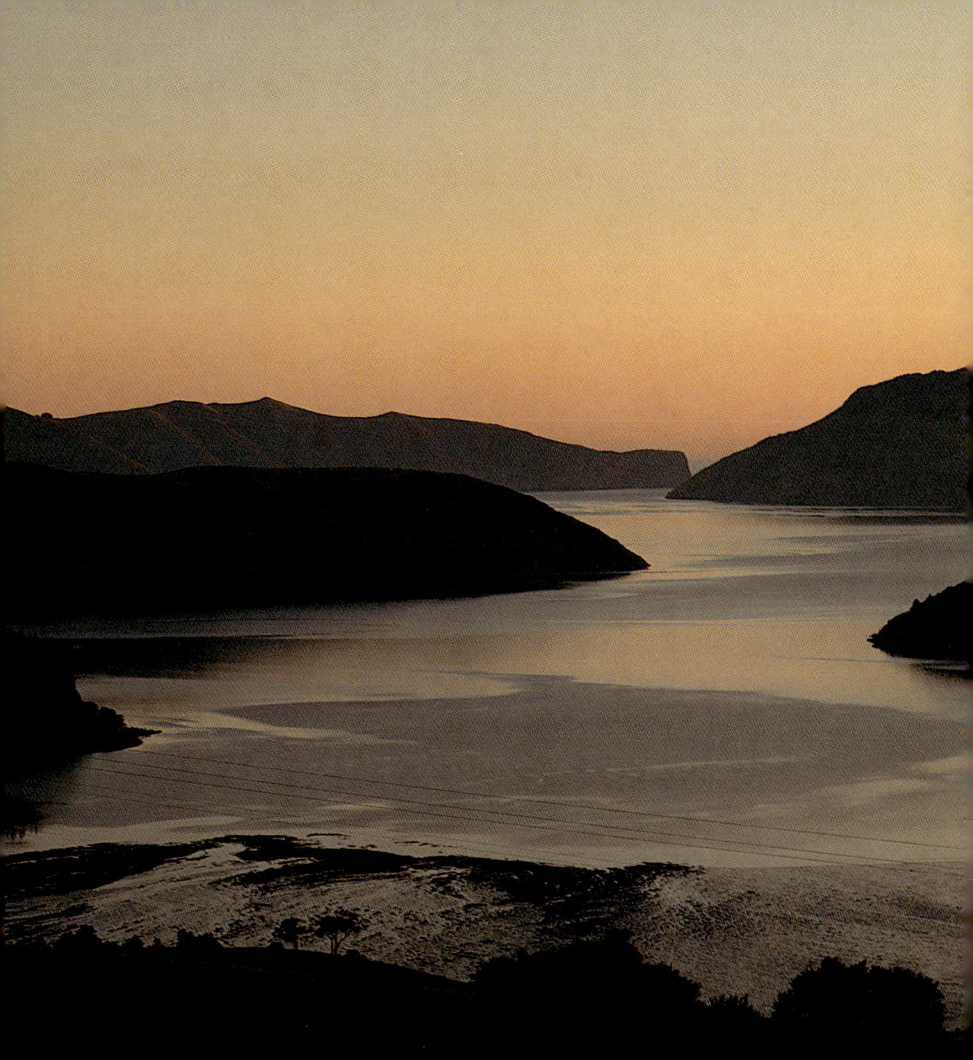

All good things
are wild and free.

HENRY DAVID THOREAU

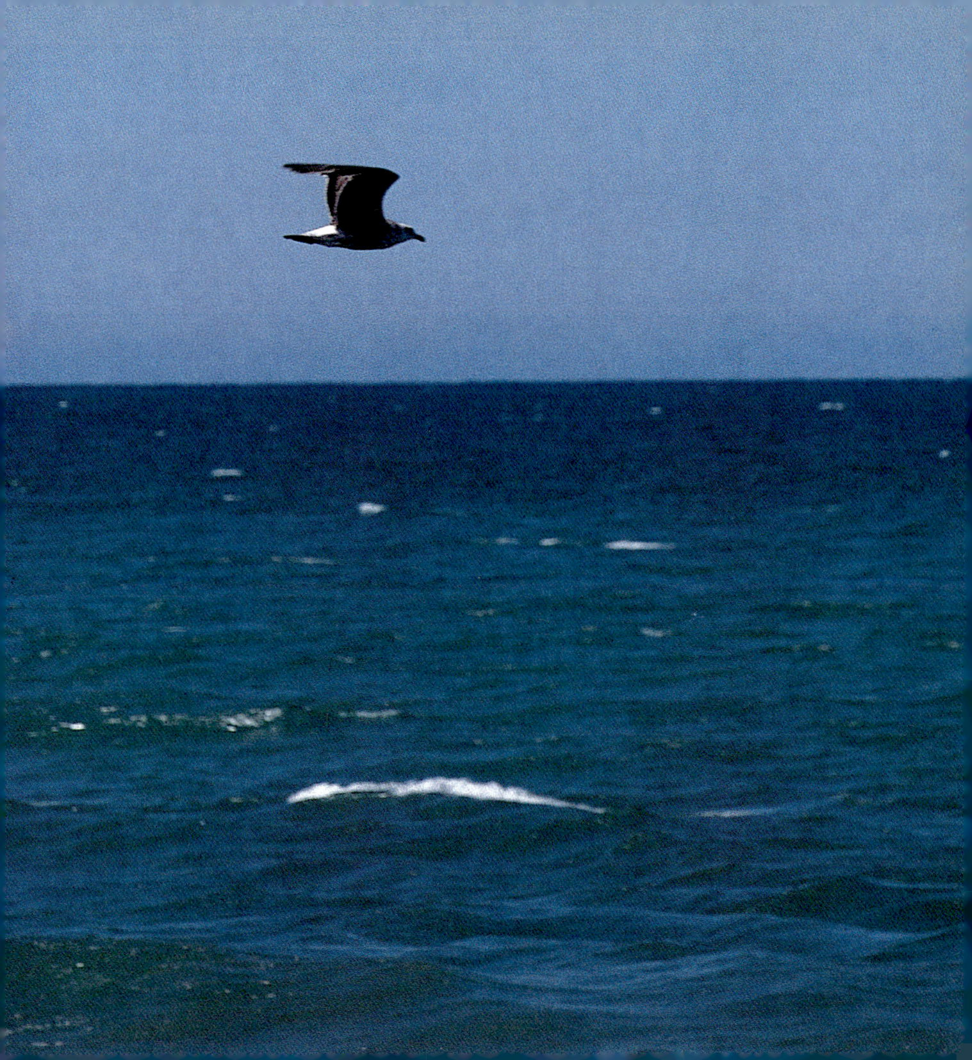

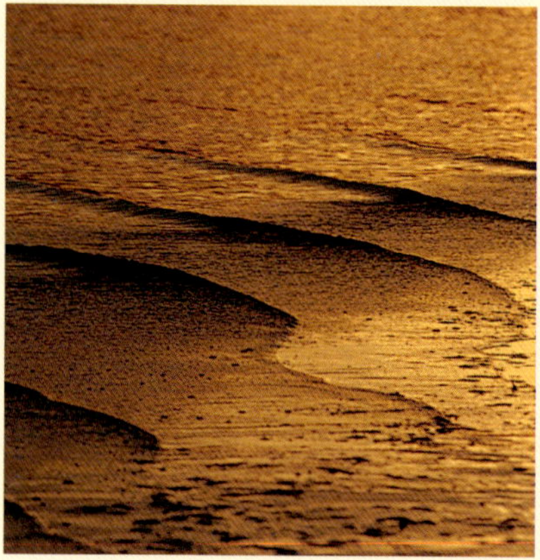

The larger the

island of knowledge,

the longer the

shoreline of wonder.

Ralph W Sockman

In the midst of winter
I finally learned there was in me
an invincible summer.

ALBERT CAMUS

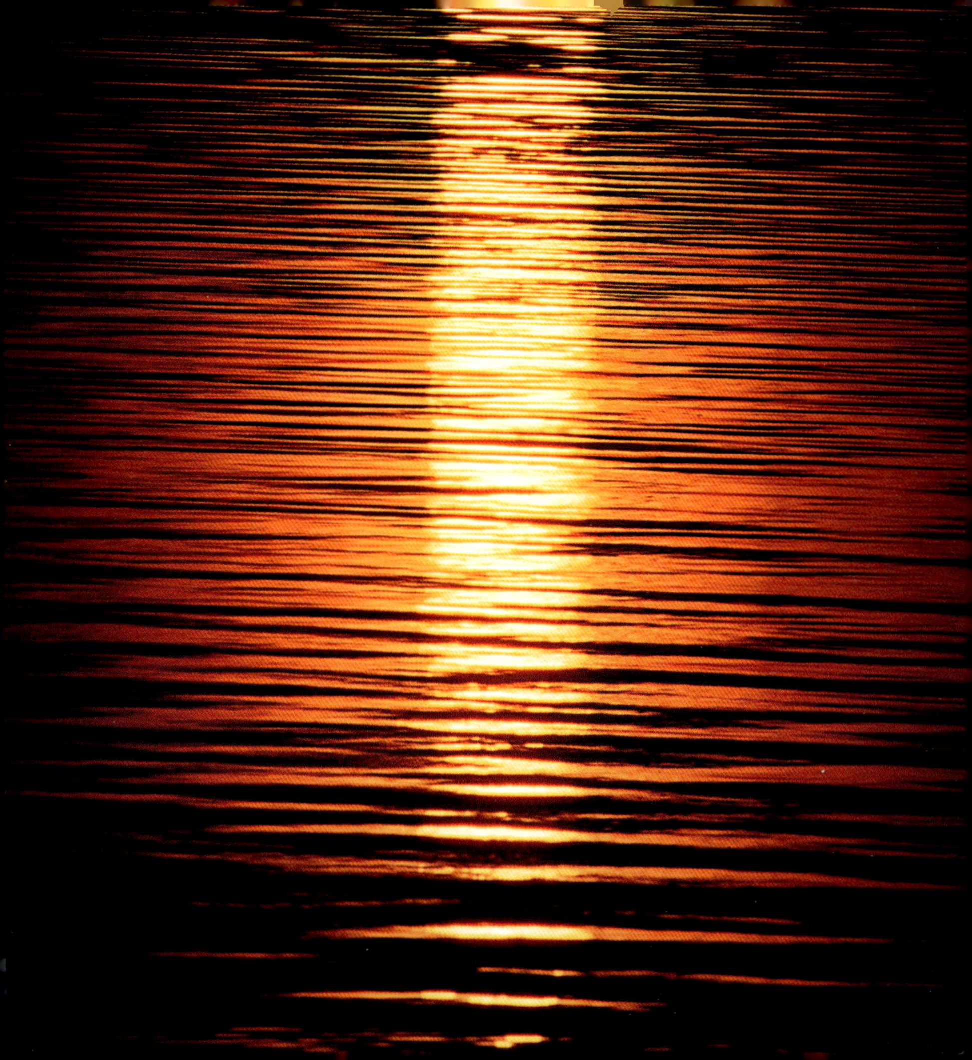

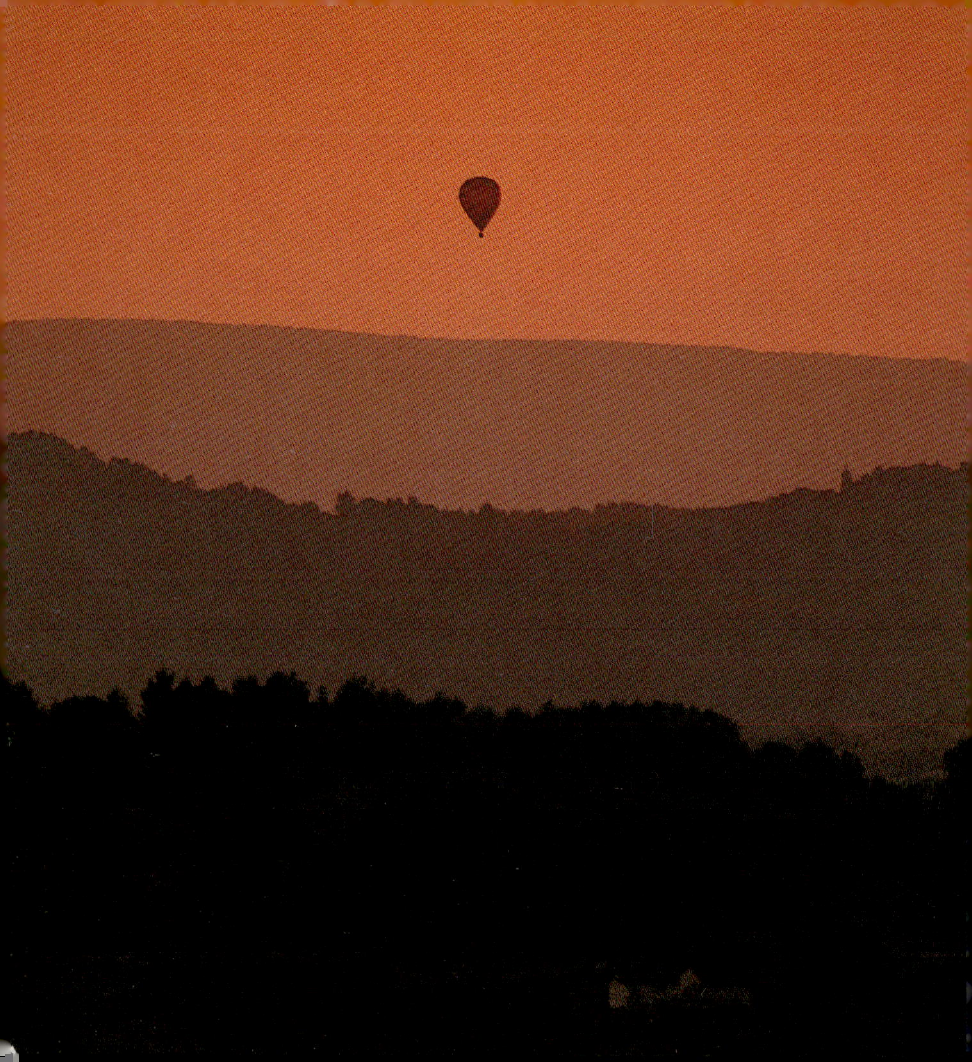

He who lives in
harmony with himself
lives in harmony
with the universe.

Marcus Aurelius

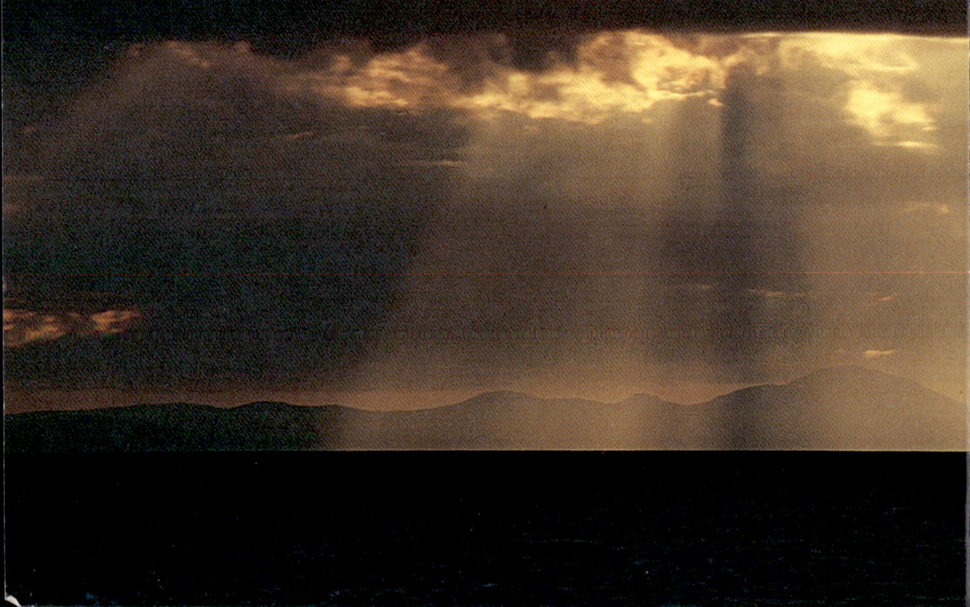

Faith is to believe
what you do not see;
the reward of this faith is to
see what you believe.

St Augustine